DEVELOP YOUR BRIDGE

I0588687

JOHN BEARD BRIDGE HOLIDAYS
13 De-La-Hay Avenue, Milehouse
Plymouth, Devon PL3 4HS
Tel and Fax. No: 01752 221072

J. C. Beard,
19 Balfour Terrace,
Devonport, Plymouth PL2 1RS
Telephone: 550838

Acknowledgements

My thanks are due to Plymouth Bridge Club and to Walter Parsons for letting us use the 'babies'; and to Robin Reynolds for photographing them.

DEVELOP YOUR BRIDGE
THE ACOL WAY

N
W E
S

JOHN BEARD

PUBLISHED BY J.B. BRIDGE COURSES

Printed and bound in Great Britain by
BPCC Wheatons Ltd, Exeter

First published in Great Britain in 1978
by Develop Your Bridge
2nd Edition 1979
2nd Edition reprint 1981
2nd Edition reprint 1982
3rd Edition 1985
4th Edition 1988
4th Edition reprint 1993

Contents

Foreword — the 'Reader'

This book is aimed primarily at the player who wants to improve his Acol Bridge. One who is almost a learner in the sense that he has been playing with rather more enjoyment than skill. Because my fundamental belief about 'THE GAME' is that it should be played for enjoyment, my aim is to increase your skill, while in no way detracting from your enjoyment.

If you usually play a hand with memories of conflicting advice running through your head; if you only HOPE you understand your partner's bidding; if you frequently lose what seemed like a certain game; if you fail to defeat the opposition's bad contract; if you sometimes make a game without really knowing why – then this book is for you.

Learn the bidding, plan the play, and know WHY you are doing what you are doing.

Eventually you will be able to forget it all again and start from scratch. That's when you start to become an expert!

Introduction to the Writer

John Beard is an E.B.U. teacher and director. As a player he is a premier regional master and was captain of Devon and Cornwall for several years. He pioneered the BB2 Bridge Programme 'Grand Slam'.

He was one of the first players to become a qualified Bridge teacher. Since then he has set many thousands of students on the road to becoming players themselves.

An Update on the Author

John freely admits that Bridge is his life and that he is a fanatic. He started the first bridge holidays and courses in this country in the early 1970's. Their (and his) popularity have grown to such an extent that he and his wife now spend most of their time organising and running Bridge holidays, in Hotels, all over Great Britain, plus some exciting venues abroad.

His holidays are formulated to create an atmosphere where one is able to enjoy their favourite game, in very comfortable surroundings, be entertained and also receive some bridge instruction.

John's first book needs no further introduction than to quote his, famous, rhetorical question:

"AFTER ALL, BRIDGE IS ONLY A GAME – OR IS IT?"

You will be delighted to know that a second book the "Conventional Way" which describes 39 simple conventions which may be used in conjunction with the 'Acol' system is available. Also a third book will be available later this year, under the title "The Play and Defensive Way".

CHAPTER 1

Opening the Bidding with One of a Suit, Why, When and What

FIRSTLY, WHY are we opening the bidding?

1. Because we want to give our partner our initial point count.
2. Because it is safer to bid at the lowest and earliest level thereby avoiding being doubled for penalties.
3. Because, if we finish the auction by defending, our bid will give our partner a guide towards a possible lead.
4. Because our entering the bidding will push our opponents to a higher level if they too want to bid.

SECONDLY, WHEN do you open the bidding?

1. When you have a hand of 14 points or more.

Example: ♠ A J 8 2
♥ K Q 6 4
♦ Q 7 6
♣ A 2

Here you bid One Heart because if your partner has Spades, he will bid them. If he shows another suit you have a natural rebid of No-trumps, showing 15–16 points. This means that a complete picture of the hand can be given on the second bid.

2. When you have a hand of 13 points. There are exceptions, however, to this rule. If you are first in hand with 3 Aces and a Jack, a Pass would be correct – as it would if you have a flat hand (4, 3, 3, 3) or are vulnerable against non-vulnerable opponents (values for One No-trump discussed later).

Example: ♠ 2
♥ K 7 3
♦ K J 10 4 2
♣ A Q 7 3

You could, of course, bid One Diamond and rebid Two Clubs.

3. When you have 12 points and a fair 5-card suit.

Example: ♠ A 2
♥ K Q 10 4 2
♦ Q J 7 6
♣ 8 6

Here you bid One Heart and your rebid would be Two Hearts or Two Diamonds.

4. When you have 11 or 10 points with one good 6-card suit or two reasonable 5-card suits.

Example:

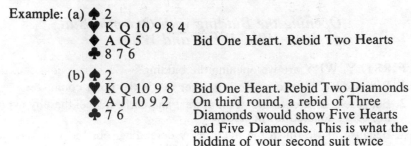

(a) ♠ 2
♥ K Q 10 9 8 4
♦ A Q 5   Bid One Heart. Rebid Two Hearts
♣ 8 7 6

(b) ♠ 2
♥ K Q 10 9 8   Bid One Heart. Rebid Two Diamonds
♦ A J 10 9 2   On third round, a rebid of Three
♣ 7 6   Diamonds would show Five Hearts
                 and Five Diamonds. This is what the
                 bidding of your second suit twice
                 shows.

5. When you have less than 10 points, only freak holdings justify opening the bidding, e.g. 7-card suits. This will be enlarged upon later in the section on pre-emptive bidding.

6. The difficult hands are the 4 4 4 1 shape. Here you must think about your rebid on the likelihood that your partner will probably bid your singleton.

Example:

♠ A Q 10 9   ♠ A Q 10 9   ♠ A Q 10 9   ♠ 4
♥ K 7 4 3   ♥ 4   ♥ K 7 4 3   ♥ K 7 4 3
♦ A Q 7 2   ♦ K 7 4 3   ♦ 4   ♦ A Q 7 2
♣ 4   ♣ A Q 7 2   ♣ A Q 7 2   ♣ A Q 10 9

Opening bid:
    1 H   1 C   1 C   1 H

These bids will give you the best chance of finding a fit at the lowest level.

FINALLY, WHAT do you promise your partner when you open the bidding at the one level?

1. Your point count is 12–19.

2. The suit you have opened in will have at least 4 cards.

3. You will bid again if you have opened one of a suit and he has not already passed.

4. If you finish by defending, your partner, if he so wishes, may lead the suit you have bid.

It should always be remembered, during the course of the bidding, that a 4–4 fit in trumps with each of you holding four in the same suit has a stronger trick potential than a 5–3 fit.

Five-card suits occur only 16% of the time and a satisfactory holding for a trump contract is one of 8 cards between declarer and dummy.

Example: ♠ A K 7 2　　　　　　　　　♠ Q J 9 3
♥ A K Q J 10　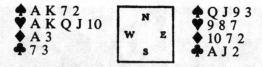　♥ 9 8 7
♦ A 3　　　　　　　　　　　　♦ 10 7 2
♣ 7 3　　　　　　　　　　　　♣ A J 2

With Hearts as trumps you can make 11 tricks. With Spades 12! (4 Spades, 5 Hearts A D, a Diamond ruff and A C). Presuming that the adverse trumps are 3–2, which occurs 68% of the time.

In trump contracts you are basically looking for 8 cards in a suit, be it 4/4, 5/3, 6/2 or 7/1, to give you the best advantage.

Remember that the most important thing is the rebid, and before you open the bidding you must always work out your rebid, allowing for all the bids your partner could make in response. You will find when you do this that you may wish to change your opening bid. If you open one suit but bid your second suit twice it would show 5 cards at least in both suits.

Before making a bid ask yourself 'WHAT IS MY REBID'.

I find it helpful on occasion to put myself, mentally, in my partner's place and ask myself how I would interpret the bidding.

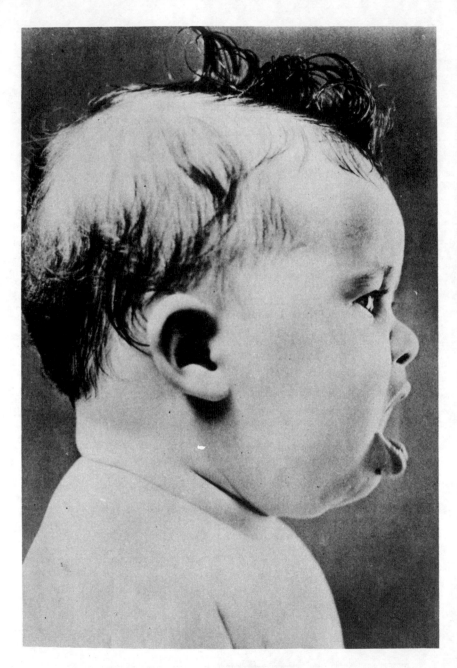

'You mean you opened on that!'

CHAPTER 2

Responses to One of a Suit

Let us assume for the purposes of this chapter that you, sitting North, have opened one of a suit.

You are saying as previously discussed that you have 12–19 points, that you will bid again, unless you receive a limit bid in response, that your partner may lead that suit and that you have at least 4 cards in it. To make discussion of the responses simpler we will suppose that you, sitting North, have opened with One Heart. East passes. Your partner, sitting South, and with no intervening bid from East, can make one of the following responses:

Responder's Bid	*Definition*
1. Any suit at the one level i.e. One Spade after opener's One Heart	6–15 points. 4-card suit in Spades or whatever suit is being bid. 6–11 points if already passed.
2. 1 No-trump	6–8 points. No 4-card major suit. Limit Bid (accurate to within two points).
3. Supporting partner's suit to the 2 level i.e. after One Heart bid Two Hearts	6–8 points. 4-card support in suit. Limit bid. No 4-card major if partner had opened Clubs or Diamonds.
4. Another suit at the 2 level i.e. Two Clubs or Two Diamonds after One Heart	8–15 points. No 4-card major but at least 4 cards in the suit bid. 8–11 points if already passed.
5. Jump bid. i.e. Two Spades over One Heart, Three Clubs or Three Diamonds over One Heart.	16+ points and is forcing to game.
6. 2 No-trumps	11 points. No 4-card major suit. Balanced hand. Limit bid.

Responder's Bid	*Definition*
7. Jump in opener's suit i.e. Three Hearts over One Heart	10–11 points. 4-card support. Limit bid.
8. Triple jump in another suit i.e. Three Spades, Four Clubs or Four Diamonds over One Heart	6–9 points mainly in suit bid. No support in opener's suit, not even 3 cards. A 7-card suit in the one being bid.
9. 3 No-trumps	13–15 points. No 4-card major. Balanced hand with no singleton or void. Limit bid.
10. 4 No-trumps	Blackwood conventional bid asking your partner for aces as a prelude to Slam (see next chapter).
11. 5 of partner's suit or 5 No-trumps	Supporting to this level is asking opener to bid 6 of his suit if he has an honour (A K Q) in it; or to bid 7 if he has two honours in his suit.
12. Game in partner's suit. i.e. Four Hearts over One Heart	This denotes a two-suited hand. Opponents are probably also two-suited. Normally 4/5-card support and 7 to 10 points in the two suits. This bid shows no interest in bidding on to a higher level. It tries to exclude the opponents to prevent them finding their fit.

CHAPTER 3

Second Bids by Opener

These bids should limit opener's hand to within two points and enable the responder to evaluate potential trick and contract value. In order to discuss possible rebids we will suppose that you had opened the bidding at One Heart and your partner had responded with One Spade. Here are your possible rebids:

Opener's Rebid	Definition
1. 1 No-trump. Or the first no trump available	15–16 points. Balanced hand. Limit bid. No 4-card support for partner's suit, if major. When playing strong NT 12–14.
2. Two Clubs or Two Diamonds	12–14 points. 5-card Hearts suit, 4-card Clubs or Diamonds. Points are mainly in the suits bid.
3. Rebidding own suit i.e. Two Hearts	12–14 points. 5-card suit. Limit bid.
4. Support for your partner's suit i.e. Two Spades	12–14 points. 4/5-card opening suit. 4-card support for partner's suit. Shape.
5. 2 No-trumps	17–18 points. No 4-card support for partner. Balanced hand. Limit bid.
6. Jump bid in another suit i.e. Three Clubs or Three Diamonds	17+ points. 5-card suit in Hearts. Forcing for one round. Could also be a waiting bid for partner to limit his hand. Does not deny a fit in his suit.
7. Jump bid in your own suit i.e. Three Hearts	14–16 points. A good 6-card suit. Limit bid.
8. Jump bid in partner's suit i.e. Three Spades	15–16 points. 4-card support in his suit.
9. 3 No-trumps	19 points. Balanced hand. No 4-card support in partner's suit if major.

15

Opener's Rebid	*Definition*
10. Triple jump in another suit i.e. Four Clubs, Four Diamonds (unusual bid)	Good two-suited hand. Not even 3-card support in partner's suit.
11. Jump into game in own suit i.e. Four Hearts	Shows an 8-card suit or solid 7-card suit A K Q J 7 6 2.
12. Supporting your partner to game in his suit i.e. Four Spades (normally majors)	17–19 points. 4-card support for partner. A hand with shape.
13. 4 No-trumps	Blackwood convention asking for Aces as a prelude to Slam bidding. Forces your partner to reply. By inference agrees to play in partner's suit.

Replies to 4 No-trumps

5 Clubs	=	No Aces or 4 Aces
5 Diamonds	=	1 Ace
5 Hearts	=	2 Aces
5 Spades	=	3 Aces
6 Clubs	=	1 Ace and void in Clubs
6 Diamonds	=	1 Ace and void in Diamonds
6 Hearts	=	1 Ace and void in Hearts

Trump suit having been agreed by inference, voids should not be shown if they are above the agreed suit, as this would force to seven, or a bad Six No-trumps.

CHAPTER 4

No Trump Bidding and Responses

There are two types of No-trump bidding. Both consist of balanced hands. There is the weak No-trump which is 12–14 points and the strong No-trump which is 15–17 points.

STRONG NO-TRUMP

I would agree with the disciples of the strong No-trump that it is a very safe bid. However, safety is not the only criteria of a good bidding sequence. In both rubber and competitive Bridge you will often find yourself bidding – and getting 1NT. However, when weak hands occur, as they frequently do, you will have to make two bids and with a strong hand you will only have to make one! Obviously this is not logical.

WEAK NO-TRUMP

I always advocate the use of the weak No-trump as the one which is likely to do the most damage to the opposition. Let us consider the reasons why:
1. It occurs five times more often than the strong No-trump.
2. With weak troublesome hands such as the 4, 4, 3, 2 distribution, one need only make one bid (1NT).
3. As it is a limit bid there is no worry about one's rebid.
4. One is saying to partner: 'I have 12–14 points, a flat hand with nothing less than a doubleton; I shall not bid again unless you force me to, either by asking if I am maximum (2NT) or by using a conventional response such as Stayman (2C) or a jump bid to the three level'.
5. It is a pre-emptive bid. It forces the opposition to a level where it may be dangerous for them to enter the bidding.
6. The danger, to the opposition, is that only the partner of the 1NT bidder has the true picture.

Examples of 1NT Opening Hands

	(1)	(2)	(3)	(4)	(5)
♠	A 9 2	A 10 2	A 10 7 2	A 10 9	A 10 9 2
♥	K 8 3	K 9 8	K 9 8	K 10 7	K 10 7
♦	A Q 9 8 2	A Q 7	A Q 6	A J 10	A 2
♣	7 2	10 9 7 2	J 7 2	10 8 7 3	J 10 7 3

Possible action by the responder

1. To leave it in No-trumps.
2. To make a weak take-out into a suit.
3. To force a game.
4. To look for a trump fit.
5. To double any overcall the opposition may have made.

1. PLAYING IN NO-TRUMPS

With less than 11 points, pass and play in 1NT because to make game you need 25/26 points. Therefore you need at least 11 points to look for game.

Example:

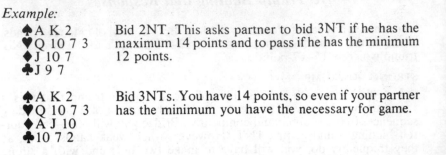

♠ A K 2
♥ Q 10 7 3
♦ J 10 7
♣ J 9 7

Bid 2NT. This asks partner to bid 3NT if he has the maximum 14 points and to pass if he has the minimum 12 points.

♠ A K 2
♥ Q 10 7 3
♦ A J 10
♣ 10 7 2

Bid 3NTs. You have 14 points, so even if your partner has the minimum you have the necessary for game.

2. *Weak Take-outs*

You make a weak take-out when the shape of your hand is such that it will play better in a trump suit. You have to remember here that you are committing the partnership to an extra trick.

Examples:

♠ Q J 7 4 2   ♠ 2   ♠ 2
♥ 2   ♥ A J 10 7 3 2   ♥ 9 8 3 2
♦ J 10 9 6   ♦ Q 7 4   ♦ A 10 7 3 2
♣ 9 8 3   ♣ 9 7 4   ♣ J 10 3

  (Bid 2 Spades) (Bid 2 Hearts)   (Bid 2 Diamonds)

As will be seen, a five-card suit is needed for a weak take-out and up to a maximum of 8 points.

3. *Forcing to Game*

This is when you know that with your partner's minimum 12 points you have the values between you for game in either 3NT or a suit contract.

Examples:

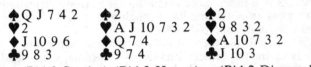

♠ A Q 9 7 2   ♠ 2   ♠ 9   ♠ 9 2
♥ 2   ♥ A Q 9 7 2 ♥ A 7 2   ♥ Q 7 2
♦ J 10 9   ♦ J 10 9   ♦ A K Q 9 7 3   ♦ 10 9
♣ A Q 7 2   ♣ A Q 7 2   ♣ 10 9 7   ♣ A K Q 7 4 3

On the first two examples you bid 5-card major at the three level – 3S or 3H. This asks the opener to choose. With three-card support he would bid 4S or 4H. With only two-card support he would bid 3NTs. In the second two examples you would bid 3NTs yourself since you do not want to play in 5Cs or 5Ds as it is easier to make 9 tricks than 11.

4. *Looking for a Trump Fit*

This is when you realise it might play better in a suit contract but have no 5-card suit.

STAYMAN (forces a reply for one round)

You bid 2C. It is a conventional bid asking opener to bid any 4-card major that he holds. If he has no 4-card major he will make the negative response, which is 2D.

Example A:

♠ A K Q 7 2
♥ J 10 9 8
♦ Q 2
♣ 7 5

Here you do not have the strength to ask for game at the three level. You use Stayman. If partner has four in Hearts or Spades you can bid game. If partner bids 2D you can bid 3S, which shows a 5-card suit and 11/12 points. If partner is maximum he can choose 3NT or 4S. If he is minimum he can pass.

Example B:

♠ A K Q 7
♥ J 10 9 8
♦ Q 7 5 2
♣ 3

You bid Stayman. If your partner does not show a fit in a major he has seven cards in the minors and it should be safe to play in NTs. So bid 2NT asking him to go 3NTs if he is maximum.

Example C:

♠ A 8 7 2
♥ 10 9 8 6 2
♦ 7 5
♣ 8 7

Although you could bid 2H as a weakness take-out you can first bid Stayman. If partner has a four-card major you would have at least 8 trumps and the lead would be going up towards the strong hand. If he bids 2D you can bid 2H and be no worse off!

Example D:

♠ A 8 7 2
♥ 8 3
♦ A K 7 3
♣ Q 7 2

After you bid Stayman, if the opener bids 2S you bid 4S. If, however, he bids 2H you then know that your weakness is filled and you can safely bid 3NTs. Also, if the opener has the other major as well, he can now bid 4S and you have not missed your fit in a major suit.

5. *Doubling an Overcall*

Since your partner has opened 1NT (12–14) you are the only person at the table who knows the true point count of each partnership. Consequently, if the opposition does bid, you are in a very strong position either to double for penalties or to pass.

CAUTION FOR THE USERS OF THE WEAK NO-TRUMP

When vulnerable against non-vulnerable opponents and first bidder, I would advise a pass on a lowly 12 points without tens and nines to give backing to your hand.

It is also wiser to pass on a hand where the points come from three aces or even three aces and a jack.

Even if you are second or third bidder, tread with caution. But when in the happy position of being fourth bidder after three No Bids, you know that the risk is much less and your partner will easily be able to assess the true position after your limit bid.

DEFENCE TO THE WEAK NO-TRUMP

With 16-plus points you double. However, if you are on lead, holding a long strong suit (7), also double. A double of a No-Trump is for penalties and should be passed unless –

♠ 4
♥ J 10 9 7 6 2
♦ K 7 2
♣ 9 8 4

you have under six points and shape such as a long suit. Here you would bid your suit.

A K Q 7 2
K 7 3
9 7 4 2
3

you know that game is on and because of the vulnerability you can make more points by bidding it yourselves than by defeating the opposition by 2 or 3 tricks (300 or 500 points). Here you bid at the three level to show your partner that you have a game going hand and asking him to choose either 3NT or to play in your suit.

Because of the effectiveness of the weak No-Trump, any overcall is always at risk. But there are hands on which you know you can make either 2C, 2D, 2H or 2S.

1	2	3
♠ K Q 7 2	♠ K Q 7	♠ K Q 7 2
♥ A J 10 2	♥ A J 10 3	♥ A J 10 3
♦ 7	♦ 7	♦ K Q 7 3
♣ A 7 4 3	♣ A 9 4 3 2	♣ 4

There are two basic systems:

TWO-WAY STAYMAN

With this system you bid 2C over the opposition's weak No-Trump, asking your partner for his 4-card major. But you must have both majors because if he does not have a 4-card major he will have to bid a 3-card major suit and you will only have 6 trumps between you.

On Example 1 you bid 2C. On Example 2 you would have to pass. On Example 3 you bid 2C.

SHARPLES

With this system you bid the minor that you hold, asking your partner to play either in that minor or in either major suit. Obviously, these take preference over the minors.

In Example 1 you bid 2C. In Example 2 you bid 2C, and in Example 3 you bid 2D.

Your Partner's Hand:

♠9 7 3 2
♥5 2   He would bid 2S
♦A K 7 3
♣9 6 2

♠A 9 3
♥Q 8 6 2   He would bid 2H
♦A 9 6 5 2
♣4

OPENING BIDS OF 2 NO-TRUMPS

This bid says, 'I have a balanced hand, no singleton or void and 20–22 points'. It is a limit bid and it is up to the responder what action he takes. He will need at least 4 good points such as K J in a suit to consider playing the game contract of 3NT. It has also to be remembered that there is no weak take-out after a 2NT bid.

Examples of 2NT opening bids:

♠A K J 10 2   ♠A K 9 7   ♠A K 7   ♠A K 7
♥A 2   ♥A Q   ♥A Q 2   ♥A 9
♦Q J 10   ♦K J 10 2   ♦K J 9   ♦A K J 7 3
♣A J 7   ♣A J 7   ♣A J 10 7   ♣J 10 2

Responses to 2 No-Trumps

STAYMAN

As after 1NT the Stayman convention can be used, asking for a four-card major if held. The bidding might go:

              2NT (opener)   3C (responder)
              3D (opener)

This would be the negative response denying a four-card major.

BARON

This is a more refined system. Here, if you have a shapely hand, you may find a fit in any of the four suits. If you are playing Baron, the signal is the same as Stayman (obviously the system you use has been determined between you and your partner beforehand). Opener replies by bidding his four-card suits upwards. With 4/5 Diamonds, he bids 3D, with 4/5 Hearts he bids 3H, and with 4/5 Spades he bids 3 Spades. If his only four-card suit was in Clubs he would bid 3NT. The responder knows that his partner has a 20–22 point count and he knows which suit he has four cards in, so he can evaluate their prospects clearly and decide on the final contract.

These are very useful systems especially if responder has a medium-size hand of approximately 11-plus points, to find a good slam in any suit and not be forced to finish in a shaky 6NT. But remember to decide on either Baron or Stayman before play!

21

Opening Bids of 3 No-Trumps

This shows a seven-card minor suit containing four honours and no more than one outside honour in another suit.

Example: ♠ K 2
♥ 9 7 2
♦ A K Q J 9 7 3
♣ 2

Responder, knowing the Qualifications for an opening 3NT bid, can:
(1) Leave it.
(2) Bid 4C, asking partner to play in whichever is his suit at the four level.

Examples:

♠ Q 9 3	♠ A 3	♠ A 5 4 3
♥ A 7 3	♥ 10 8 6 5 3	♥ A K Q 10 6
♦ 8 2	♦ 8 6 3	♦ 8 2
♣ Q 6 5 4 3	♣ 8 6 3	♣ K 4
Bid Pass	Bid 4C	Bid 6D

Opening Bids of 4 No-Trumps

This is a conventional bid asking for aces. If you have one ace you bid that suit (with Ace of Diamonds bid Diamonds). If you have none, you bid Clubs (with Ace of Clubs you bid 6C). With two aces you bid 5NT.

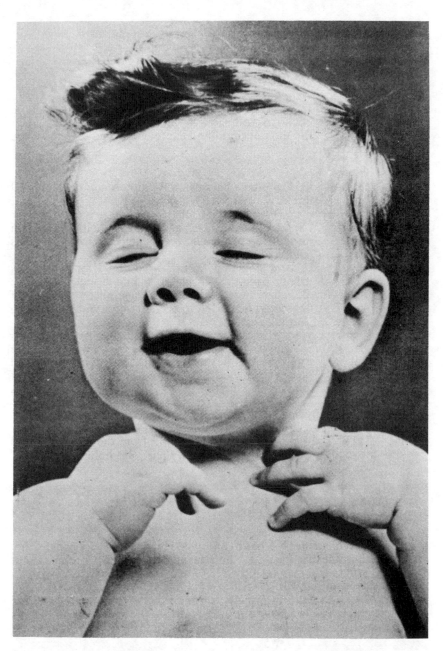

'You can see now why I prefer the weak No-Trump.'

CHAPTER 5

Assessment of Final Contract

Since the opener's first bid shows a point count of 12–19 his second bid should reduce this count to within two points. Hence, the responder should be able to clarify their position and appreciate whether game is on, or only a part score.

GAME CALLS

Three No-trumps	25–26 points between the partners are needed, as 9 tricks are required for game.
Four Hearts or Four Spades	Approximately the same number of points but length in the trump suit can be counted, as can singletons and voids:– 1 for a singleton, 2 for a void and 1 for each extra trump over the 4. These should bring you to the 25–26 required for game. Remember that none of these can be added to a point count until the trump suit is agreed.
Five Clubs or Five Diamonds	As can be appreciated, 11 tricks must be made to be successful in these contracts. It has to be considered that, with a good 5-card minor, one may be better off playing in Three No-trumps (9 tricks instead of 11).

After a limit bid, by opener or responder, the other is in a better position to evaluate in which contract they should play.

e.g. 1H – 1NT. The opener has had a limit bid from the responder and knows exactly, to within 2 points, what their joint holding is worth.

Example 1: ♠ K Q 7 5
               ♥ A K 9 2   One Heart
               ♦ J 2
               ♣ Q 8 3

Opener's hand

Responder's hand on 1NT has 6–8 points. Here, the opener can see that his best bid would be 'Pass', as their combined maximum total cannot exceed 23 points and may be only 21. Game is not possible and so, with his balanced hand, he will leave it in 1NT.

Example 2: ♠ A K 10 9 7 6
               ♥ K J 6   One Spade
               ♦ Q 7 2
               ♣ 5

Opener's hand

24

Responder's hand on 1NT has 6–8 points. In this case the opener will rebid Two Spades, as this hand will obviously play better in a trump contract and the responder should have nothing worse than a doubleton in his suit. Now responder must pass as he has made a limit bid.

Example 3:

♠ A K 7 4
♥ K J 3
♦ A 5 2
♣ K 9 8

} One Spade

Opener's hand

Responder's hand on 1NT has 6–8 points.

As opener here you have 18 points. If responder has the maximum 8 you want to bid 3NT. To discover whether he is minimum or maximum, you bid 2NT. If he has 6, he will pass. With 8, he bids 3NT.

The same principle applies should it be the opener who has limited his hand on his second bid. His limit bid, of 1NT (or 2NT if that is the first available NT bid), shows a point count of 15–16. Therefore, if responder had 10 points it is apparent to him that the partnership has the necessary 25–26 needed for game.

Nine tricks can be made and with a flat distribution, 3NT is the bid he will make.

The response of No-trump bids are very accurate, limiting the hand as they do and completely 'painting the picture' for the partnership. Either opener or responder can be in no doubt about what their final contract should be.

When opener rebids another suit without limiting his hand.

i.e. opener 1♥   responder 1♠
      opener 3♣

The responder's responsibility now is to describe his point count as closely as possible. In the example the opener's rebid is a forcing bid, a jump showing 17+ points.

A simple sign off, at the lowest level, by responder shows 6–8 points. Opener was looking at least for game and possibly Slam, which would need 12 tricks.

If the bidding had gone:–

      opener 1♠   responder 2NT
      opener 3♥

the opener, having received a limit bid from the responder, which shows him 11 points, now says, with his Three Hearts, 'We have a choice of playing this hand in either of three contracts. If you have 3-card support it would be Four Spades. If you have 4-card support it could be Four Hearts. If your 11 points have Two Spades, Three Hearts, Four Diamonds and Four Clubs, bid Three No-trumps.'

This illustrates how vital it is to tell each other the complete story, if you are to arrive in the correct contract; and how helpful limit bids are in this connection.

Remember, that even with 13 cards in one suit, you still have only 10 points! 'Shape' is what counts. With a hand of good shape and a trump suit agreed upon, your values for game can be less than they need to be when in a No-trump contract.

In a later chapter we will have more to say about the play of both the trump contract, and the No-trump one.

SLAM BIDDING

A small Slam is the making of twelve tricks. A Grand Slam is the making of thirteen tricks. For both of these one scores extra bonus points.

It is usually after one of the following, that a partnership contemplates bidding a Slam:–
1. Opening 2♣ and receiving a positive response.
2. When the bidding has confirmed that a pair has 32/33 points for a small Slam, and 35/36 for a Grand Slam. You will check that you have controls, of course.
3. A shapely hand where you have two supported suits between you, and are looking for controls.
4. After a strong bid, i.e. 1♠ – 3♣ or ♦. This shows 16+ points. If opener has a hand of strength himself (17–19 points) or a hand with playing strength, he will contemplate a slam.

Example: *Opener's hand*

♠ A K J 10 7
♥ Q J 10 2
♦ K 3 2
♣ 9

If bidding has gone 1♠ – 3♥ you could now be interested in Six or Seven Hearts.

To discover your joint controls you bid Four No-trumps (Blackwood). This asks your partner how many Aces he holds.

Responses: 5♣ = 0 or 4
5♦ = 1
5♥ = 2
5♠ = 3

If the Four No-trump bidder then bids Five No-trumps he is asking for Kings. But, in bidding Five No-trumps he is showing that the partnership have all the aces between them.

Responses to Five No-trumps are virtually the same as those to Four No-trumps.

6♣ = 0 or 4
6♦ = 1
6♥ = 2
6♠ = 3

26

CHAPTER 6

Opening Two of a Suit

There are occasions when you are dealt a hand which is very large in point count and is a hand of power and quality. You know immediately that, with so many points in your hand your partner will be unlikely to have many. It is necessary, therefore, to open the bidding with a bid which compels your partner to reply, irrespective of his point count. This is known as a forcing bid.

The Acol Conventional bid is an opening bid of Two Clubs. You do not need to have a Club in your hand to make this bid! What you are saying is that you have game in your own hand or 23+ points.

Example:

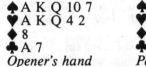

♠ A K Q 10 7   ♠ 8 4 2
♥ A K Q 4 2   ♥ 9 3
♦ 8   ♦ 9 7 6 3 2
♣ A 7   ♣ 9 7 4

Opener's hand   *Partner's hand*

Opener's hand has at least 10 tricks, but he does not know which of his suits as trumps will guarantee him 10 tricks. He needs to know in which of these suits his partner holds 3 cards. He is not, at this stage, interested in the point count, only the suit support. Since his partner's hand is a hand without points, a Yarborough, he would normally make no response, but an opening bid of Two Clubs forces him to answer.

The negative response to a Two Club bid is Two Diamonds, so this is what the responder in our example would reply. This denies either 8 good points or an Ace and a King. A positive response would be anything but Two Diamonds. Either Three Clubs, Three Diamonds, 2NT, Two Hearts or Two Spades. If the suit which you wanted to respond in was Diamonds, then you could have bid Three Diamonds, and to show Clubs it would have to be Three Clubs.

With a flat distribution, no 5-card suit and wishing to make a positive response, you would bid 2NT.

In our example the bidding would go: –

Opener		*Responder*
	2 Clubs	2 Diamonds (negative)
(shows suit)	2 Spades	2NT (second negative)
(shows 2nd suit)	3 Hearts	3 Spades (showing preference for Spades)
(Game bid)	4 Spades	

Until Game is bid, after a Two Club opening, the bidding MUST be kept open. The only exception to this occurs in the following bidding sequence: –

Opener	Responder
2 Clubs	2 Diamonds (negative)
2NT	

This shows 23–24 points and a flat distribution and asks for 3NT if any support at all, but it can be passed with under 3 points.

In the sequence: –

Opener	Responder
2 Clubs	2 Diamonds (negative)

Three No-trumps shows 25/26 points and a possibility of making 9 tricks in No-trumps.

Here openers have to remember that unless their partner has some values in his hand to allow them to get into it, they will continually be leading away from strength, which makes it very difficult to make 9 tricks with 25–26 points in one hand only.

OPENING TWO OF A SUIT OTHER THAN TWO CLUBS

In the Acol system these bids are used as strong bids signifying that, with a certain suit as trumps (Diamonds, Hearts or Spades), you can make 8 playing tricks – or more.

Normally, you would have a good 6-card suit. Frequently the reason for opening 2 of a suit is, that if you only opened 1, there is no way, on your rebid, of describing your hand with accuracy.

Examples:

(a) ♠A 2
♥A K J 10 9 7 2
♦K 2
♣9 2

(b) ♠A Q J 7 5 2
♥A J 10 2
♦A 2
♣8

The (b) is not a true 8 tricks. However, if you opened One Spade, how are you going to describe your hand accurately? Would One Spade with a rebid of Three Hearts be misleading? Yes, the better way is to open Two Spades. Your subsequent bidding is then much more certain, both for you and your partner. He understands at once that you have 8 playing tricks and will have a picture of the shape of your hand. He knows the level at which to stop the bidding, and so will you, after the set response from your partner.

RESPONDERS' REPLIES TO OPENING TWOS OF A SUIT
(FORCED TO BID FOR ONE ROUND)

1. If the responder changes the suit he is promising at least One Ace and One King in his hand, although not necessarily in the same suit: –

e.g. 2♠ – 3♣
or 3♦
or 3♥

2♠ – ♠7 3 2
♥A 9 7 5 2
♦K 3 2
♣Q 2
} Bid Three Hearts

28

2. If he supports the opener's suit he must have 1 Ace and at least 8 points with 3-card support: –

   e.g. 2♥ – 3♥   2♥ –   ♠7 3 2 5
   or 2♦ – 3♦   ♥A 9 7 5   } Bid Three Hearts
   or 2♠ – 3♠   ♦Q 7 2
                                 ♣Q 2

3. If he jumps to game he has no Aces, 8 points and at least 3-card support in an opener's suit: –

   e.g. 2♦ – 5♦ (3NT   2♥ –   ♠7 3 2
        may be better)   ♥K 9 7 5 2   } Bid Four Hearts
   or 2♥ – 4♥   ♦Q J 2
   or 2♠ – 4♠   ♣Q 7

4. If he bids Three No-trumps he has a flat distribution, 8–11 points and a doubleton in opener's suit: –

   e.g. 2♠ – 3NT   2♠ –   ♠7 3
                                 ♥K 9 7 5   } Bid Three No-trumps
                                 ♦Q J 2
                                 ♣Q J 7 2

5. If he bids Two No-trumps, this is the negative response stating that he holds *none of the above values.*

CHAPTER 7

Defensive Bidding

One of the best defensive bids we have in the Acol system is the No-trump opening bid (12–14 points). Firstly because it is pre-emptive, forcing the opposition to a higher level. Secondly because, if you have bid 1NT, your partner is the only one who knows the combined point count of the opposition. By adding his own points to your opening 12–14 he is aware of the exact value of the opposition's holdings and can tell whether he can defeat their contract.

Example: ♠J 8 7 3 2
♥A 6 3
♦Q 9 2
♣K Q

Here you have 12 points. Is your Spade suit worth a rebid? NO, the hand is only worth one bid. A lot of people forget this point. Instead of blindly opening One Spade and having your partner bid two of another suit, it might be more descriptive on this holding to bid 1NT. At least it would have the same pre-emptive value and in any case you really do not want spades led in defence; it would be better for your partner to find a natural lead. But it is bad policy to hide a good 5-card major.

A good way of giving information to your partner through defensive bidding is by using: –

Overcalls. For instance, when the opposition has opened One Heart you overcall One Spade. This tells your partner that you have at least **5 cards in Spades**, it shows a point count minimum of 10 and a maximum of 14, and also gives him a lead indication. Should your point count and values be stronger than this, you have a choice of two bids as overcalls.

With 13–16 and a 6-card suit you jump the bidding, i.e. One Heart from opener and you bid Two Spades. With 16+ points you double the initial opening bid and rebid your own suit after your partner has replied to your double. We will say more of this later. But let us now consider defensive overcalls by having a look at some hands.

Example 1: ♠A K J 9 2
♥Q 2
♦7 5 4
♣6 4 3

Obviously you would not open the bidding on this hand. But if the opposition has opened in front of you and you can still bid at the one level, you will want to show your partner that he can lead Spades and that you have some defensive tricks to your hand. You would bid One Spade.

Example 2:
♠ A Q J 7 3
♥ 7 4
♦ A 9 8
♣ 10 6 2

Here again you could open One Spade (values are a little light), because you just have a rebid of Two Spades which would show 12–14 points and a 5-card suit, but a simple overcall in Spades would be better if you can bid later on in the auction at the one level.

Example 3:
♠ A K J 10 6 2
♥ A 2
♦ Q 7 3
♣ 9 4

This hand is too strong for a simple overcall because if your partner only has 7 points (Ace and King) then there must be a play for 10 tricks and game. Therefore a better way of describing this hand when overcalling would be to jump the bidding, i.e. One Heart by opener, Two Spades by you to show a good six card suit and 13–16 points.

CHAPTER 8

The Sixth Suit – the Double

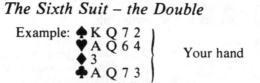

Example: ♠ K Q 7 2
♥ A Q 6 4
♦ 3
♣ A Q 7 3   Your hand

Suppose the opposition had opened first with One Diamond. What are you going to bid on the above hand?

If you overcall in a suit you are immediately promising your partner that you have 5 in it, so you cannot bid One Spade, One Heart or Two Clubs. Here you use what I call the sixth suit. This is the double, i.e. One Diamond from opener and double from you. This would be saying, 'I have an opening bid but I have not got a 5-card suit', or it could be saying, 'I have a strong hand.' Subsequent bidding will distinguish which of these you have.

Assume now that you are sitting in West place. Your partner at East place has doubled North. The bidding has gone: One Diamond – Double – No Bid – you.

Since you are *forced* to reply to a double, when there has been no intervening bid, we will go over the seven possible responses you can make.

1. With less than 8 points simply bid your 4-card suit.
2. Bid One No-trump on a balanced hand, 1½ covers in opener's suit and 9–10 points. The strong point count, basically, is because your partner inferred he does not want to play it in No-trumps. He wants to play in one of the other three suits and you are denying him a fit in a suit.
3. With 9–10 points and shape, jump in your 4-card suit, especially if it is a major suit. This is not a forcing bid and your partner may pass if he has doubled with a fairly weak hand and shape.
4. With 12+ points bid opener's suit. This is game forcing and asks partner to clarify hand.
5. With a good 5- or 6-card suit and 9–10 points you double jump. If your suit is a minor one, you must seriously consider playing in Three No-trumps, rather than bid at the 4 level. It may be better, if you have no stop in opener's suit, to devalue your hand and bid 3 only.
6. You bid Game, with 10–13 points and a 6-card suit. Again, it must be a good suit and again, consider playing in Three No-trumps, if it is a minor one – especially with 1 stop in opener's suit.

DYB - C

33

7. Pass for penalties. Vulnerability needs to be considered. If you are vulnerable and the opposition are not, it needs to be remembered that they have 600 points to play with, if you can make Game, before you make a profit. So think carefully before leaving a double.

Doubling, on the whole, at the one level, is for suit finding, and leaving a double in, is usually not worthwhile.

Examples:

(a) ♠ Q 9 7
♥ A J 3 2
♦ 9 5
♣ A Q 3 2

What would you do if the opposition had gone One Diamond and your partner had doubled?

Here you do know that, with your 13, you have the point count for Game between you. Inform your partner of this fact by bidding the opposition's suit – Two Diamonds.

(b) ♠ 9 7 2
♥ 8 5 4
♦ J 7 3
♣ 10 7 3 2

Again your partner has doubled One Diamond. What do you bid?

You are obviously not strong enough to go to the 2 level so, in this instance, you are going to have to lie to your partner (a thing I never like doing!) by bidding the cheapest bid available. Here it would be One Heart or One Spade. What you cannot do is pass. If, however, you partner had doubled One Spade your bid would have to be Two Clubs.

(c) ♠ A J 10 2
♥ 7 2
♦ K Q 7 2
♣ 7 5 4

Your partner has doubled One Heart.

Your bid in this situation is Two Spades, showing your partner at least a 4-card suit and 9–10 points.

(d) ♠ K 7 2
♥ A 10 7 3
♦ Q J 9 4
♣ 10 2

Your partner has doubled One Heart.

You have 10 points, so you tell your partner that you have 1½ covers in their suit by bidding One No-trumps, describing the hand accurately.

(e) ♠ 7 2
♥ A Q 9 8 7 2
♦ 6 2
♣ 9 5 2

Your partner has doubled One Heart. You cannot pass quickly enough – for penalties! But say your partner had doubled One Diamond – One Club or One Spade?

This is a difficult one. You are really not good enough to jump to the 2 or 3 level. Yet you are far too good to just bid One Heart over the opening bid. As your partner has doubled, I think you could say Two Hearts and hope that your partner has not doubled on a 2-suited hand.

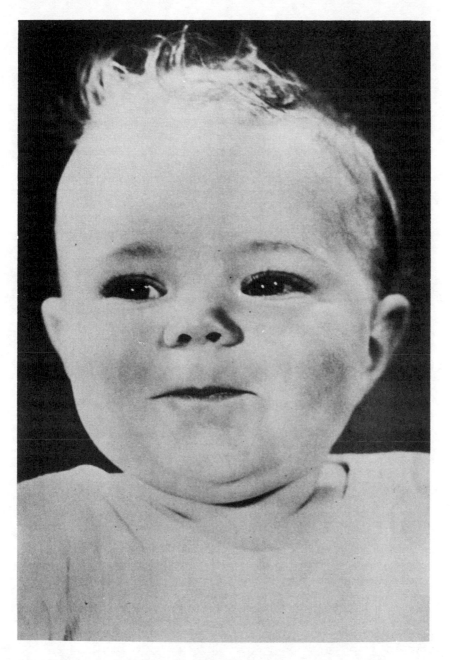

'I double.'

CHAPTER 9

Countering the Double

Now we will consider the other side. If your partner had opened one of a suit, e.g. One Heart, and been doubled by the opposition, what do you do? There are six possible responses.

1. Pass. Without 3-card support, and with less than 6 points, do not rescue partner, even if you have a singleton. The possibility is that, even though the opposition have trumps between them, your partner might still make 7 tricks with his outside hand.
2. Support partner to the 2 level, with up to 6 points and 3-card support.
3. Support partner to the 3 level with 7–9 points and 3-card support. Personally, with only 7 points, I would like 4-card support, but it would not be wrong if the vulnerability was in your favour, i.e. non-vulnerable against vulnerable opponents.
4. Bid Two No-trumps, showing 11 points and 4-card support in partner's suit. It would have been a normal raise to level 3 if opposition had not doubled.
5. Bid Game showing a weak hand with 5-card support and shape. The opposition might also be shapely and could make Game in another suit so this is pre-emptive.
6. Redouble. You have 10+ points and only 2 cards or less in partner's suit. Generally, your partner will pass any response by opposition, to see what action you are going to take. Here you are looking for penalties. Often, you can use this bid to warn partner that you have no support in his suit. Remember that the double is saying, 'I have the other three suits.' You are looking for the best contract and in some cases it will be more profitable to defend than to play.
7. If you have none of these requirements ignore the oppositions double and make a natural bid.

Example 1:   ♠A 7 3 2   Your partner has bid One Heart and been
            ♥4 3 2   doubled.
            ♦9 8 7
            ♣7 3 2

You have 4 points and 3 cards in his suit. You would support to Two Hearts.

Example 2:   ♠3 2   Again your partner has bid One Heart and
            ♥9 8 7 2   been doubled.
            ♦A 7 3 2
            ♣K 5 4

You have 7 points and a 4-card support. Here you would immediately jump to Three Hearts. If the opposition have a spade fit you don't want them to be able to find it at a low level!

37

Example 3: ♠ A 7 6 3   Once more your partner has bid One
♥ A Q 7 2   Heart and been doubled.
♦ 3
♣ J 10 8 4

Here you would bid 2NT because you have a normal raise to Three
Hearts. In this particular example, with a singleton Diamond and a good
control in Hearts, my partner's suit, I would be awaiting his rebid, because
I know that we have at least Game in Hearts. We might even have a possible Slam if he can show any other suit but Diamonds, i.e. One Heart –
Double – 2NT – Pass – Three Clubs or Three Spades (showing you a
second suit which fits your hand). You would then agree his second suit
by bidding Four Clubs or Four Spades, but the final contract must be left
to him, as you will have then given a complete picture of your hand.

He would bid Three Hearts if he had opened weak (12–14).

He would bid Four Hearts if he were stronger (14–16).

Example 4: ♠ A763   Once more your partner has bid One
♥ 72   Heart and been doubled.
♦ J43
♣ K1084

Just make your natural bid of One Spade. Partner will now limit his
hand and you will be able to evaluate the best contract.

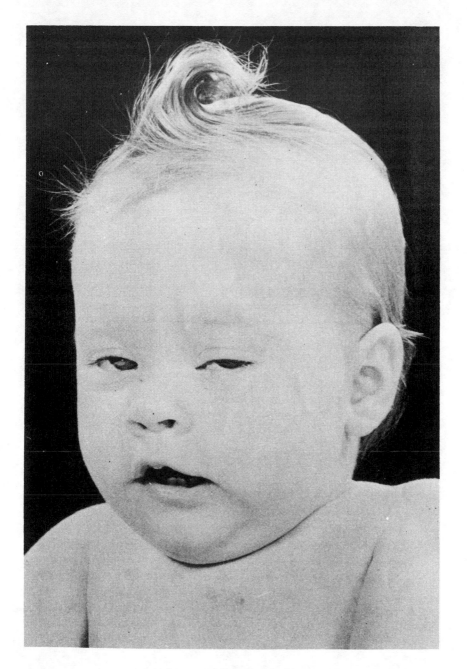

'. . . and I redouble.'

Doubling The Opener

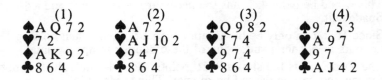

	(1)	(2)	(3)	(4)
♠	A Q 7 2	A 7 2	Q 9 8 2	9 7 5 3
♥	7 2	A J 10 2	J 7 4	A 9 7
♦	A K 9 2	9 4 7	9 7 4	9 7
♣	8 6 4	8 6 4	8 6 4	A J 4 2

We will assume for the purposes of the test that the opposition have opened the bidding with One Diamond. You, sitting in second place, have doubled, and there has been no bid from the third player. Which of the above hands does your partner hold?

(a) on bidding One Spade; (b) Two Diamonds; (c) Two Spades; (d) 1NT; (e) Two Hearts.

RESPONSES WHEN YOU OR YOUR PARTNER HAVE BEEN DOUBLED

You are the opener now and have bid One Heart. You have been doubled. Which of the following hands does your partner hold?

	(1)	(2)	(3)	(4)
♠	A 7 3 2	A J 10 2	K 7 2	7 2
♥	4 3 2	7 2	A 10 7 3	A Q J 8 7 2
♦	9 8 7	K Q 7 2	Q J 9 4	6 2
♣	7 3 2	7 5 4	10 2	9 5 4

(a) On bidding Two Hearts; (b) Three Hearts; (c) 2NT; (d) On a redouble; (e) One Spade.

ANSWERS TO TEST ON DOUBLING THE OPENER

(a) This could be Hand 3. One Spade implies a weak hand with a maximum of 8 points and probably a 4-card Spade suit.

(b) Since a Two Diamonds bid is bidding the opponent's suit, it means your partner is looking for Game. Hand 1. You could finish in 3NT but at this stage your partner does not know the shape of your hand.

(c) This would be hand 4. It has the necessary 9–10 points and a 4-card Spade suit.

(d) Since 1NT can only be bid in answer to a double, when holding 1½ honours in opener's suit, none of these hands are appropriate!

(e) The Two Hearts bid shows 9–10 points and a 4-card suit. It is non-forcing and can be passed by opener. This is Hand 2.

ANSWERS TO TEST ON RESPONSES WHEN YOU OR YOUR PARTNER HAVE BEEN DOUBLED

(a) Hand 1. Maximum of 6 points with 3-card support.

(b) Hand 4. Your partner would have had a difficult decision, however, on this hand. Whether he bid Three Hearts or Four Hearts would really depend on the vulnerability.

(c) Hand 3. 11 points and 4-card support. It would have been a good raise to Three Hearts, without the intervening double.

(d) Hand 2. 10 + points with a doubleton in your suit.

(e) None of the hands really warrants this bid!

CHAPTER 10

Pre-emptive Bidding

What is pre-emptive bidding?

It is a bid that shows a hand of unusual shape, normally a 7-card suit. The pre-emptive bidder opens the bidding, at the 3 level, in that suit.

A simple rule of thumb is to look at a hand and count your losers, before you make a pre-emptive bid. Roughly, this means the missing Aces, Kings and Queens in each suit.

Example 1: ♠ A J 9 8 7 6 4   Example 2: ♠ A J 9 8 7 6 4
            ♥ 7   ♥ 7
            ♦ Q 2   ♦ J 10 3 2
            ♣ K 3 2   ♣ 8

In Example 1 there are 7 losers (two in Spades, one in Hearts, two in Diamonds and two in Clubs). By definition, a 7-loser hand is a 6-winner hand!

In Example 2 there are also 7 losers and 6 winners (two in Spades, one in Hearts, three in Diamonds and one in Clubs). This too, in spite of the differences, is a 6-winner hand.

The main reason for the pre-emptive high opening bid is to keep the opposition out of a Game or set them up for a penalty double by your partner. He knows exactly what you hold.

The logic behind the pre-emptive bid is the assumption that the opposition have the values for Game. Your own hand will be useless in defence. However, the other assumption that you must make is that you will be doubled! To make allowances for this probability, the vulnerability is of vital importance.

If we take our examples again, we find that they are 6-winner hands; since they are bid as Three Spades we should find ourselves three light, doubled. Has it been worth it? The following table may help you to know the pros and cons.

Points We Give Away	*Points We Score*	*Do You Open?*
Non-vulnerable versus non-vulnerable:		
500	400 in duplicate	No
	100–400 in rubber	
	(both approx.)	
Vulnerable versus vulnerable		
800	600 in duplicate	No
	600–800 in rubber (approx.)	

Points We Give Away	*Points We Score*	*Do You Open?*
Vulnerable versus non-vulnerable:		
800	400 in duplicate	No
	100–400 in rubber (approx.)	

Non-vulnerable versus vulnerable:		
500	600 in duplicate and rubber	Yes
	or 800 in rubber (approx.)	

Although it appears to be safe to pre-empt on only one of the four possible vulnerabilities, we must not forget that we have a partner. The easiest way to remember, is to recall that when vulnerable you need a 7-winner/6-loser hand: when non-vulnerable you need a 6-winner/7-loser hand. If you stick to this rule you should stay out of too much trouble.

Your partner, knowing the above, and checking the vulnerability, has a good idea what is required from his hand to make Game. If non-vulnerable it needs 4 top tricks (Aces and Kings) in his hand to make Game. If vulnerable, 3 top tricks are needed. He has to remember that the opener is already showing a 7-card suit and only one card is needed for support to give the 8-card trump fit.

DEFENCE TO PRE-EMPTIVE BIDS

Over the years I have tried various defences, but I have yet to find the ideal one. However, I will list a few, and would suggest that partners discuss the matter to ensure that both of you are using the same defence.

1. **The optional double.** This leaves 3NT and suit calls as natural bids, but should be left in when you have the trump suit.
2. **Fishbein or Herbert.** You bid the next suit up, requesting your partner to take the bidding out into his suit. 3NT is natural.
3. **Lower minor.** You bid the lowest minor available, requesting your partner to take it out into his suit.
4. **Reese.** You bid 3NT over majors and double the minor. Doubling the majors is for penalties.
5. **F.I.L.M.** This is a combination of Fishbein and lower minor. It keeps the bidding lower, over Three Diamonds or Three Hearts.

    It will be seen from these that a pre-emptive bid is a very good weapon if used properly.

    The opposition always have the feeling that you are trying to put one over on them, and frequently reach too high a contract in their attempts to stop you!

CHAPTER 11

Planning the Play

After the opening lead and exposure of dummy, the first thing declarer should do is thank his partner – as though he means it! Never criticize either your partner's bid or a final contract. The only thing you would be doing by this is alerting the opposition that you are either too high or in the wrong contract.

For the purposes of discussion we will assume that you have the following hands: –

♠J 8 4 2
♥Q 5
♦9 8 3
♣A K J 10

West leads Six Clubs

♠K Q 10 9 3
♥A K 2
♦K 6 2
♣7 2

You are South, having reached a contract of Four Spades, West has led the Six Clubs.

As declarer what are your thoughts – what should they be?
 1. Where are my losers?
 2. Where are my winners?
 3. Can I make my winners before the opposition make theirs?
 4. Can I safely get rid of any of my losers – perhaps on a second suit?
 5. Is there a safe hand, a hand which I can allow to take the lead?
 6. Is there a danger hand, which I do not want on lead?
 7. Can I trump in with the short trump suit and make myself extra tricks?
 8. What information has the opponents' bidding given me?
 9. Can I afford to finesse (remembering that finesses have only 50% chance of success)?
10. Can I give myself the best chance by remembering that with 5 cards against me in any suit they will break 3/2 68% of the time, 4/1 28% of the time (1 hand in 4)?
11. Can I give myself the best chance by remembering that with 4 cards against me they will break 3/1 50% of the time, 2/2 40% of the time, and 4/0 10% of the time?
12. If I decide on a cross ruff will I be able to make enough tricks?

13. If I must take a finesse, can I take it as late as possible by which time I will have all the information I need to increase my chances of success?
14. Can I force the opposition to make their critical decisions as early as possible, before they receive full information from their partner?
15. What information has the lead given me (the size of the card)?
16. Are we in the right contract? If playing duplicate, is it the same contract as everyone else? This could make a difference to the number of tricks you may need to get a good result.
17. Can I play my cards in such a way as to give as little information as possible to the defenders (i.e. with choice of A K Q J in a suit I will take the trick with A or K since I have no partner I could deceive by so doing).

All these points should be considered even before you play the first trick. With practise this does not slow down the game. It actually speeds it up due to your having formulated a plan upon the first round of the way the hand is going to be played. However, flexibility is still necessary once playing has begun.

Now let us play the hand, keeping the above 17 points in mind. There are 10 potential winning tricks.

There are 4 potential losers. The danger hand is East because he, when on lead, can lead through your King of Diamonds and if West has the Ace then you will lose 3 tricks in Diamonds.

Method: Take the first trick with the ♣A followed by three rounds of Hearts, throwing the ♦3 from North's hand. Now lead your trump. If East has ♠A and switches to Diamonds, then the opposition can only make two tricks in Diamonds. You will thus make your contract.

MISTAKES THAT LEARNERS MAKE

1. Failure to draw trumps and thereby letting opposition make tricks by trumping your winners. Trumps should be drawn 90% of the time.
2. Failure to appreciate that, when playing in a 5/3 trump fit there is no advantage, nothing to be gained, by trumping in with the long trump hand, until you have trumped in three times. Even then you are only making one extra trick, assuming a normal break against you in trumps.
3. Drawing trumps before taking any opportunities available of ruffing in with the short trump hand.
4. Drawing opponents' outstanding master trump when it entails using two of yours.
5. Being afraid to lose a trick, even if, by doing so, you will be able to make more.
6. Playing a suit in the wrong order and cutting yourself off from winning tricks in one of the hands, i.e. A K 9 7 2 in one hand and Q 8 4 in the other. Playing the A K first will cut you off from the hand.
7. Taking all your winners too quickly, and then wondering where the rest of the tricks are coming from. It will be too late by then! You have lost control.

8. Hasty play to the first trick, before having formulated a plan.
9. Being over-keen to open a new suit. This applies to both declarers and defenders. If you have Q 7 2 opposite J 8 4 the chances are that if you are first to lead this suit will make no tricks.
10. Not finessing, even though you still must lose a trick in that suit later.
11. Not leading towards top honours, once, or even twice if necessary, i.e. K 9 2 or K Q 5.
12. Not recognizing the best opportunities of making extra tricks, i.e. with five trumps outstanding they will break 3/2 most of the time.
13. In a tricky contract, not taking your tricks while you have the chance.
14. Not realizing that, if you are looking for extra tricks, they come from establishing a long suit in No-trumps or a second suit in a trump contract.
15. Not remembering, when playing in No-trump contracts, that it is a race to make your long suit before the opposition can make theirs. Therefore you must not play their suit and set up their winners for them.

CHAPTER 12

Making Your Contract

THE NO-TRUMP CONTRACT

It has been said that a hand is harder to play in a No-trump contract than in a trump one. It is true that you do, in No-trumps, have less control over the situation. It is therefore essential to remember, in No-trumps, that it is a battle for tempos. A race, if you like, for the establishment of your long suit before any suit in which the opposition may have length.

Careful planning is even more important when the dummy hand goes down. Even greater emphasis has to be put on the need for entries. Where are your winners? COUNT YOUR TRICKS. For 3NT you need nine and you must count at the beginning to see where these are coming from.

One of the first weapons at the disposal of declarer is the hold-up play. This is designed either to put the lead on the safe hand or to exhaust one of the opponents in that particular suit – thus making his hand safe. Take the following examples: –

Example 1:

9 2

K Q 10 4 3 | N W E S | 8 6 5

A J 7

You are North and South as declarer and dummy.

If West leads the K and you refuse to take the trick, West can no longer lead that suit without giving you two tricks. He has to play into another suit, and might easily be setting the second suit up for you whilst you still have control of the first one, presumably the one they, as opponents, are trying to make. You have gained a tempo advantage.

Example 2:

9 8 7

Q J 10 5 2 | N W E S | 6 3

A K 4

Again you are playing as declarer and dummy at North and South.

If Queen is led, you can refuse to take the first trick. When you take the second trick you have made East a safe hand. Not only that, but it is now necessary to get in, for West, not once but twice, and if he has sufficient to do this he would have had an opening bid.

The only danger with this hold-up is that you may have a weaker suit which you do not want attacked. In which case it might be beneficial to take the first trick and hold up on the second trick – still making a hand safe. Only the rest of your hand will tell you which play is safe.

Example 3:

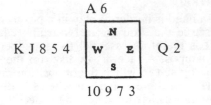

A 6

K J 8 5 4   Q 2

10 9 7 3

You are N/S once again.

The lead from West is the 5. Most declarers would duck this trick and play a 6 from North. But they should work out why West has led a small card. If he had King and Queen and Jack he would have led the King. Assuming that West has five in his suit and East has two, you play the Ace. If East puts a high card on your Ace, to unblock the suit, he gives you a trick with the 9 or 10. If he plays small, when he is in with his honour, he will block his partner's suit and cannot lead back. If he plays small and his partner overtakes an honour with an honour, again your 9 or 10 will make. So, in this instance the correct card on the first round is the Ace.

Example 4:

3

Q 8 4   A 10 9 7 6 5

K J 2

You are N/S.

During the auction East has bid this suit. West leads a small one. This marks him with an honour. If, on the second round, you put in the King, if West unblocks with the Queen, your Jack makes. If he doesn't, he can only play the Queen and has to get his partner in on another suit before they can establish this one. It is a race!

Bearing such points in mind marks the difference between the beginner and the expert player. Like most subjects, as soon as you think you are beginning to learn it, the realization comes of how much you still need to know!

One basic difference between the experienced and the beginner is that the former can count up to 13! Sometimes four times in one hand, once for each suit! However, do not despair. A large part of such an ability comes simply from practising – and from motivation and concentration.

However, I hope that you won't start out by trying to count every hand, although later in this chapter I shall be giving you one to try. Although not wishing to make yourself unpopular at the table by taking too long, do try to work out some of the opposition's holdings. Remember that experts are those who know which distribution is probable and use these probabilities. Thereby providing themselves with the best possible chance of making their contracts.

TRUMP CONTRACTS

For our example we will assume that you, at North, started with this hand: –

      ♠10 9 2
      ♥8 7 3
      ♦J 10 8 6 4 2
      ♣2

South has: ♠A K Q 5 4
         ♥10 9
         ♦–
         ♣A K Q 10 9 8

The opposition have bid Hearts but you have won the auction, eventually finishing in Four Spades. The opposition lead three rounds of Hearts, and you trump in on the third round, from South. Most declarers would now draw trumps.

It is true that on most hands trumps should be the first line to examine. In possibly 90% of cases one should draw trumps. Sometimes, however, this policy must be rejected. Knowing this, may be the first sign that a player is beginning to get above average – he is beginning to understand his winners and his losers. When playing a two-handed suit it is usually correct to establish, or at least to explore, the side suit before drawing trumps. You can probably cope with a bad distribution of 4/1 in one suit and/or 4/2 in the other, against you, but you should try to cover at least one and if possible, both probabilities.

So, in our example, three rounds of Hearts have been played and you have trumped the third round. If you then immediately draw trumps and the distribution is 3/2 against you (which occurs 68% of the time) then all is well. But, with five cards against you a break of 4/1 (28%) is possible. If it does, then you might not make your contract because you have already lost two Heart tricks. Should such a distribution occur you could now lose One Spade and One Club. Recollect that with an even number of cards in a suit against you, they are likely to break evenly, i.e. 2/4 with 6 cards. With an odd number they are likely to break unevenly, i.e. 2/3 with five cards.

51

In our example, the best way to guard yourself is to play a high Club on the fourth round. Next a low Club and ruff on the table. Now even with a 4/1 break in trumps against you, you can afford to have the Clubs break 4/2, the probable distribution. So, think before rushing into the standard procedure of playing a hand; THINK, THINK, THINK, both about probable distribution and about the opponents' likely holdings.

CROSS RUFFING

Let us now consider a cross ruff. Whenever you have shape, such as in our last example, where Diamonds and the Clubs can be ruffed, it is a method which bears examination.

The first thing you must do on a cross ruff possibility is to count the number of tricks you are going to make. Do not, just because you have a singleton in each hand, embark on a cross ruff because it is the first line of play that springs to mind. First, see if you can make sufficient tricks this way for your needs, and secondly, cash your side winners as early as possible. Thirdly, trump the latter rounds of a suit with as high a trump as you can afford, and fourthly watch your timing carefully. Remember that while you are trumping high the opposition are discarding cards, and they may then be short-suited in a suit where you had controls and have forgotten to take them in the early stages. One trap you must not fall into!

Take the following example. It is mid-play in a Diamond contract.

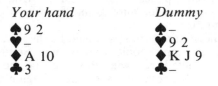

Your hand
♠ 9 2
♥ –
♦ A 10
♣ 3

Dummy
♠ –
♥ 9 2
♦ K J 9
♣ –

You will see that you have five rounds to play. You are playing a cross ruff and you have, quite correctly, used your side winners earlier in the game. When you lead from Dummy with the ♥ 9, do not make the fatal mistake of trumping with the ♦ 10. You must use the Ace. After leading a small Club or Spade back, trump in with the ♦ K. By doing this it simply does not matter who has the ♦ Q. The opposition can take one trick with the ♦ Q BUT – and this is the most important point – when they do take it, if they play a second round of trumps they cannot now do damage by drawing a trump from each of your hands.

During a cross ruff, never forget, when you get down to the last five tricks, that most of the cards the opposition has left are trumps! Or they are short-suited as well and can over-ruff. Your top winners, Aces, etc., must have been taken before you get to this position.

REVERSE DUMMY PLAY

This is not as frightening as it sounds. Here, set out below, is a hand to illustrate reverse dummy play.

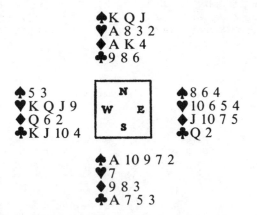

♠K Q J
♥A 8 3 2
♦A K 4
♣9 8 6

♠5 3
♥K Q J 9
♦Q 6 2
♣K J 10 4

♠8 6 4
♥10 6 5 4
♦J 10 7 5
♣Q 2

♠A 10 9 7 2
♥7
♦9 8 3
♣A 7 5 3

Your contract is Four Spades. You are South and you are playing the hand. West leads the ♥ K and you count your tricks. You can see Five Spade tricks, One Heart and Two Diamonds and One Club – calamity, only 9 tricks!

Now take a mental walk around the table and look at the set-up from dummy's point of view. If you can trump three times in your long trump suit then you can make one more trick. So you take the first trick with the ♥ A. Then trump another Heart, lead a Diamond and trump another Heart with the ♠ 10, lead a Diamond to the King and trump another Heart with the ♠ A. Now cash the ♣ A, and draw trumps with the King, Queen and Jack. South has no more trumps (YOU) and on the ♠ J the losing Clubs or Diamonds can be discarded. The contract is there.

Always bear in mind that you need to trump, when in a 5/3 trump fit, three times with your long trumps before you make yourself an extra trick.

'I can't remember how many trumps are out.'

CHAPTER 13

Defensive Play

Defensive play is the area where thinking, real thinking, counts most of all.

There are far more mistakes made in defence than in declarer play! Frequently the declarer who is uncertain of his contract can relax and let the defence make it for him!

Good defence depends, above all, on trust between partners. The opportunities which arise for you to help each other fall into four main categories: –

1. *Bidding for a lead;* directing your partner to play a suit.
2. *The opening lead;* i.e. when you have had no indication from your partner of what he would like you to lead.

After the exposure of dummy: –

3. (a) *The leader can now plan his subsequent defence;* and (b) *The third player plans his opportunities* on the basis of what he can see in dummy and the deductions he makes from the size of his partner's lead.
4. *Information given from cards played* by the other half of the defence team as discards, following suit, etc.

Remember that mistakes made in defence can seldom be corrected, as declarer has the balance of the points. This is why playing in 1 NT, Two Clubs, Two Hearts or Two Spades is so difficult. The hands are so balanced that the defenders have more time to correct their mistakes, through being on lead more often.

1. BIDDING FOR THE LEAD

It is sensible to make a competitive bid just to give a lead indication to your partner. He would then have to have a good reason NOT to lead your suit to you. Possibly the subsequent bidding would show that it might not be worthwhile. Therefore, if you bid, you must have strength in the suit and want it led.

Example 1: ♠A K 7 5 2
♥7 3
♦Q 7 2
♣Q 7 2

You could make an opening bid here. It would be better to make an overcall. Since you want a Spade led, bid One Spade.

Example 2: ♠A Q J 7 2
♥7
♦Q 7 3 2
♣9 5 2

In this hand there's no hurry to bid your Spades because if your partner hasn't bid he would be the only person you would be deceiving. If he has passed you could make an overcall, even though you have only 9 points. It would give a lead indication.

57

Example 3: ♠ 9 2 ♥ K Q J 7 3 ♦ A 7 3 ♣ 10 3 2	A lot of people would fall into the trap of making an opening bid on this hand. You do not have the Spade suit, and the only thing you might do is help the opposition to get into a possible Spade fit.
Example 4: ♠ 10 3 ♥ K Q 7 2 ♦ A 7 3 ♣ K 10 9 3	Here again, you have 12 points and if the opposition open One Spade in front of you, it may pay you to double, if the vulnerability is favourable. It would let your partner know that you can stand a bid in the other three suits or that, if you defend, he can make an attacking lead.
Example 5: ♠ A K Q 2 ♥ J 8 7 3 2 ♦ 7 2 ♣ 6 5	If you are going to bid there is only one suit to mention – Spades! Your Heart suit is not worth showing. I would treat this hand as a 4/4 hand with shape, and bid the higher ranking first.

There is also the method of doubling a system bid or of response to a system bid, i.e. Blackwood, Stayman, Flint or Gerber. These can be used to give your partner an indication of the suit you would like him to lead.

2. OPENING LEADS

These are very important. In high level contracts they will often be the means of making or breaking. Perhaps the easiest way of choosing a lead is by use of the simple mnemonic APT.

A stands for Attacking
P stands for Passive
T stands for Trumping

Example:

You are North. Here is your hand.

♠ Q 9 2
♥ K Q 10 2
♦ J 7 2
♣ A 5 2

First of all you ask yourself, 'How did the bidding do? What did it tell me?'

For instance, if the bidding went One Club, One Spade, Two Spades? Or if it went One Spade, No Bid, Two Spades, No Bid, No Bid? What would that tell you?

East, as opener, has showed 12–19 points. But he did not show any further interest after his partner's reply. Therefore he has a minimum hand of 12–15 and/or he must have shape because he did not open One No-trump. He is either weak, with shape, or has 15/16 and does not wish to go any further upon hearing that his partner has 6/8 points only.

It is on this deduction that you must find your lead against two spades.

(a) **Attacking lead.** This is where you lead either from an honour or with an honour, hoping that your partner has another honour in the suit. In our example you could lead the ♣A as an attacking lead. But, with the ♥K you can not only make a safe lead but also an attacking lead. Sometimes, an attacking lead can also be a passive lead when you have a sequence from which you lead the highest.

(b) **Passive lead.** A passive lead, on this hand, is a low Diamond. I would really like a little less in this suit. We could lose a trick or the tempo if partner has such holdings as Q 8 2 or K 8 2 or 10 9 2.

Examples:
K Q 10 2. Lead the King	A K Q. Lead the Ace
A K 4. Lead the Ace	A J 10. Lead the Jack
K J 10. Lead the Jack	Q J 10. Lead the Queen
K Q J. Lead the King.	A K only. Lead the King

(c) **Trump lead.** This is leading either a trump or a short suit such as a singleton or a doubleton. In our example we could lead a trump to deny declarer's cross ruff, but we might lose a trick if we did, so it would not be a good lead. Remember that if you are leading a short suit, your partner must be able to get in to give you a ruff.

If you have four trumps with a top honour it might be better to lead a long suit. You want to make declarer trump in with his long trump hand because you could then, eventually, finish with trump control. With small trumps their trick value is in drawing declarer's trumps, in order to prevent him ruffing, or by using them to ruff in yourself.

3. (a) PLANNING THE DEFENCE AFTER THE EXPOSURE OF DUMMY

Now let us suppose that you have led the ♥K, a safe, attacking lead of top of sequence. Dummy goes down. Now you can mentally work out what your partner holds. In dummy you can see 7 points. With your 12 that is 19. Which leaves 21 points between declarer and your partner. Since you have already deduced from the bidding that declarer has 15–16 at most, your partner should have 5–9 points.

Across the table, what is your partner thinking?

(b) He too can see dummy's 7 points. Since he knows that he himself has 7, that makes 14. He places his partner with 10–12 points. Since the ♥K has been led he deduces that his partner (you) has led from a sequence. If this is so, he thinks, then you will probably have 5 points in the Heart suit and 5/6 in the other suits.

He now has to make up his mind whether to encourage or reject the Heart suit. The size of the card he plays will tell you which he is doing. This is information passed and is the most important part of the defence. Since declarer has the balance of the points the information passed to one's partner must be accurate. Do not try to be clever in order to deceive declarer. He can see 26 cards. The person you will deceive is likely to be your partner.

4. INFORMATION GIVEN FROM CARDS PLAYED

There are four ways to signal information to your partner during play.
(a) **Petering.** This is playing high-low. You could follow suit by playing first the 8 and then the 2. It shows an even number of cards in the suit and asks your partner to continue that suit. Perhaps you have got one of the top honours or have a doubleton and want to ruff in on the third round. If you peter in the trump suit it shows your partner that you still have a trump and, what is more important, that you want to ruff in.
(b) **Playing the seven or above.** This encourages your partner to continue the suit. If it is a discard then you are asking for that suit to be played at the first opportunity. Unless it is obvious that it is the lowest card in your holding. In which case you can confirm that you do not want this suit, by throwing away a higher card on the second round.

Remember, when signalling, to use the highest cards that you can afford. If you have A K Q and you only need one or two tricks to defeat the contract, signal with the Ace! At least your partner will wake up! If you played the 7 and partner can see, between dummy and himself, 2 3 4 6, you can hardly blame him for not realizing you want the suit led!
(c) **Playing fourth highest in a suit.** At third place, your partner subtracts the card led, away from eleven and works out what declarer's holding in that suit is likely to be, i.e. the lead is Six Spades. Dummy holds 10 8 2 and you are holding A 9 3. Eleven minus six = five. You can see four cards higher (A 10 9 8) than the one led. So declarer has only one card higher. This is particularly useful information when defending against No-trump contracts.
(d) **McKinney Signals**

1. ♠7 3   or 2. ♠7 3
   ♥A K 9 7 2   ♥A K 9 7 2
   ♦A 7 2   ♦9 4 2
   ♣9 4 2   ♣A 7 3

You are defending against a Spade contract. You lead ♥A and your partner encourages you with ♥8, showing he has either ♥Q or a doubleton. You play ♥K and he plays ♥3. You will now be playing a card for him to ruff (or win with his honour). The card you play is very important. The size of it indicates to him which of the other two suits you would like him to lead back – other than trumps, of course. From hand 1, you would now lead the ♥9 since you want a Diamond led and Diamonds are the highest of the two remaining suits. On hand 2, you would lead the ♥2 since you want a Club led and Clubs are the lowest. he then leads back the suit you have indicated. Thereafter, you might be able to give him a further ruff, or over-ruff or destroy a certain trick for declarer and a possible discard for declarer if one of his hands started with Q J xx.

TRUMP PROMOTION

If your partner leads a card which declarer is obviously going to over-ruff, he is asking you to ruff with your highest trump. The reason could be that by over-ruffing declarer could promote trump tricks in your partner's hand.

IMPORTANT POINTS

Assume cards in partner's and in declarer's hands.

Always make things easy for your partner. Do not give him a chance to go wrong. Do not signal to your partner that you have an Ace unless it is necessary for him to know, because you are also giving information to declarer.

Last, but not least, remember that your partner is on your side, believe it or not! Do not tell him lies, do not deceive him or feed him inaccurate information. If he/she does all that to you it will depend what sort of person you are whether you turn the other cheek – or change your partner! Divorce seems a serious step, but after all you do want to be a good Bridge player – don't you?

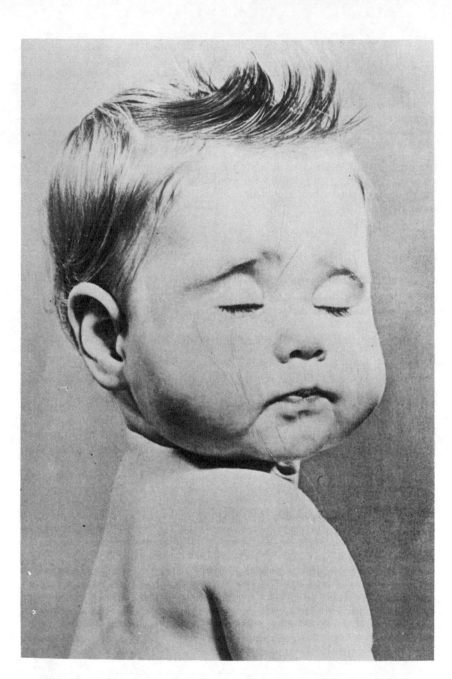

'That's quite enough. I don't want to hear any more about it.'

CHAPTER 14

Duplicate Bridge

Many players prefer Duplicate to Rubber Bridge because the element of luck is largely removed. And with it the frustration of sometimes sitting all evening with poor hands.

Success at Duplicate is due to your ability to achieve more tricks than all the other pairs who will be playing the same hands.

The hands are preserved as they are played so that each deal can pass unchanged to the next table. Eventually every East/West pair will have played the full set of East/West hands and each North/South pair all the North/South hands. As can be imagined, players can enjoy themselves comparing their own contract and results with those of the other pairs!

The scoring is adjusted to take account of the fact that each deal is a separate entity. In addition to normal Bridge points a part score earns 50, a vulnerable game 500 and a non-vulnerable game 300. Apart from there being no credits for honours, all other aspects of scoring are unchanged.

The boards (wallets of dealt hands) are put on the tables at the commencement of each round. A simple system of marking indicates the vulnerability of each pair and which of the four is the dealer for that board.

At the end of the game the cards are replaced in the wallet in the same order.

Scoring is done by means of a travelling score card which moves on with the board. At the end of a session all the boards are collected and the marking is done by the director in charge.

The minimum number of players able to play Duplicate is 8, as two teams of four. When playing in teams, half the team would be in the East/West position and the other half in the North/South, and scores are added on the same board at the end of the session.

Find yourself a friendly event and give it a try. You'll be surprised how much you enjoy it!